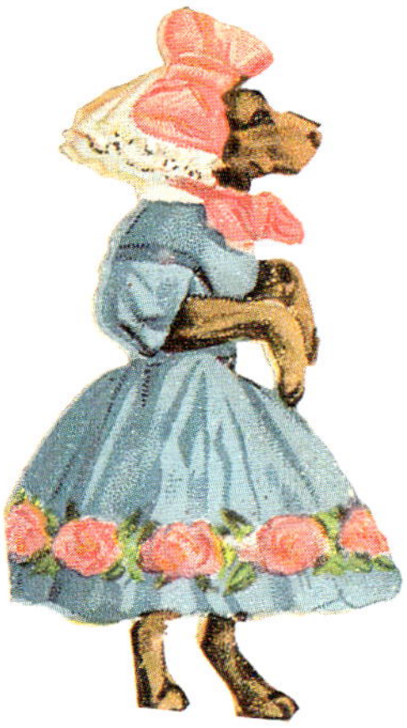
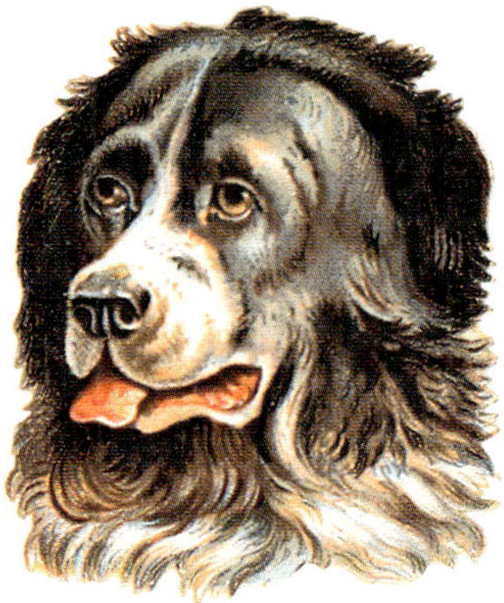
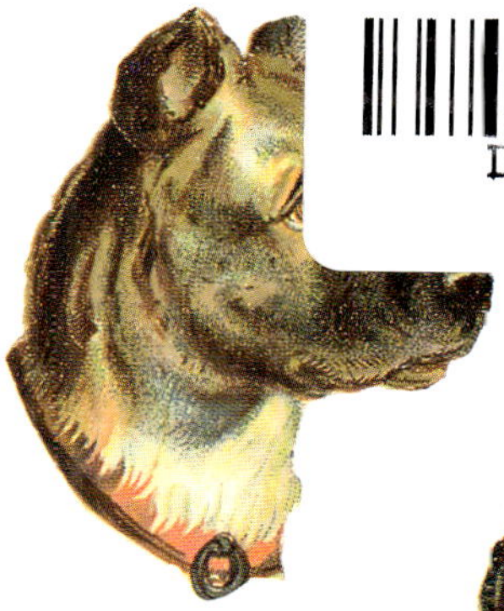
D1829255
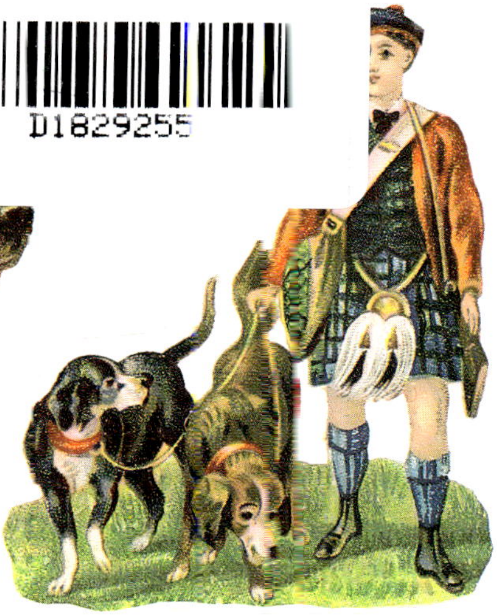
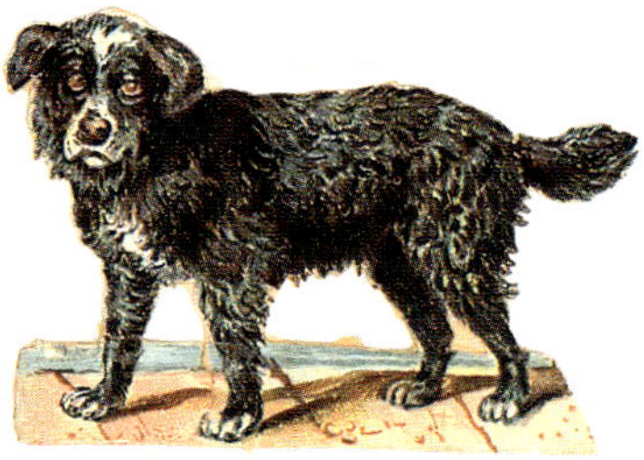
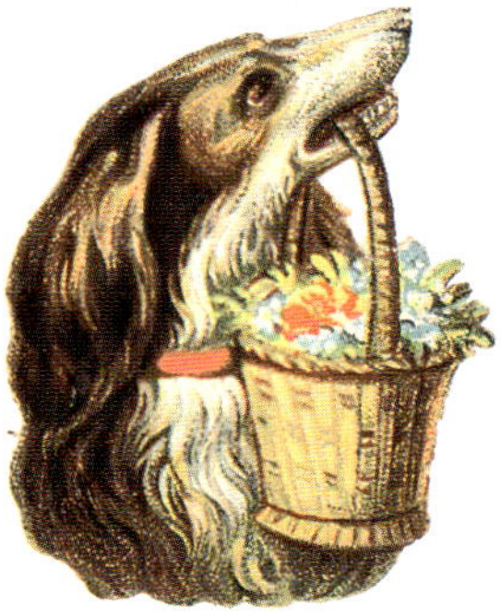
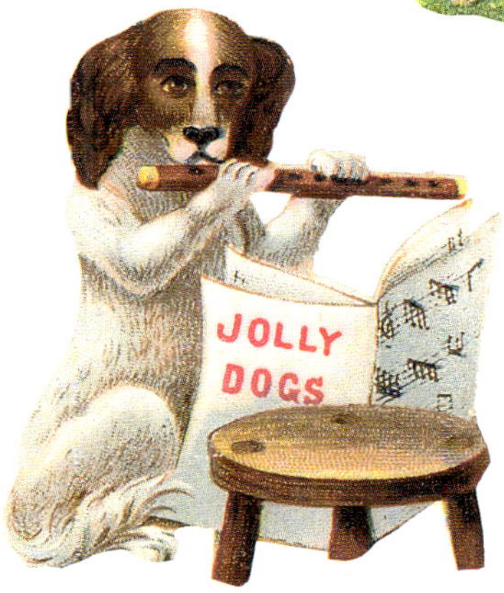

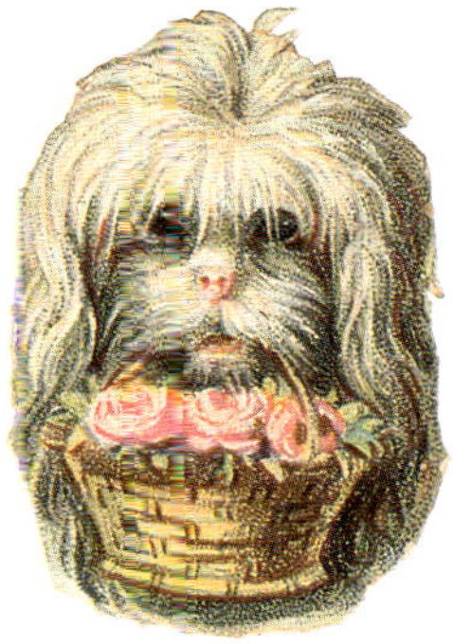
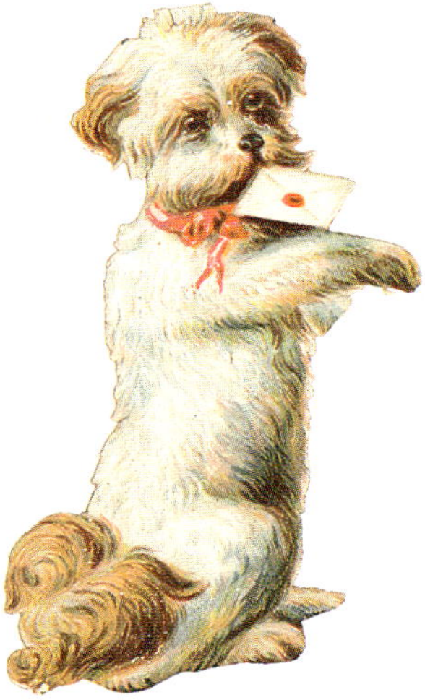
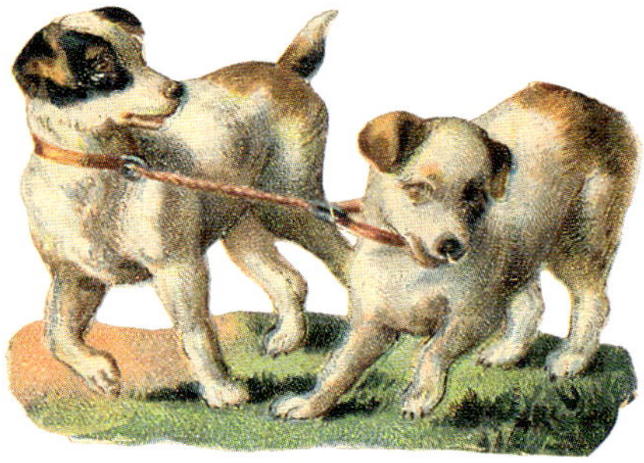
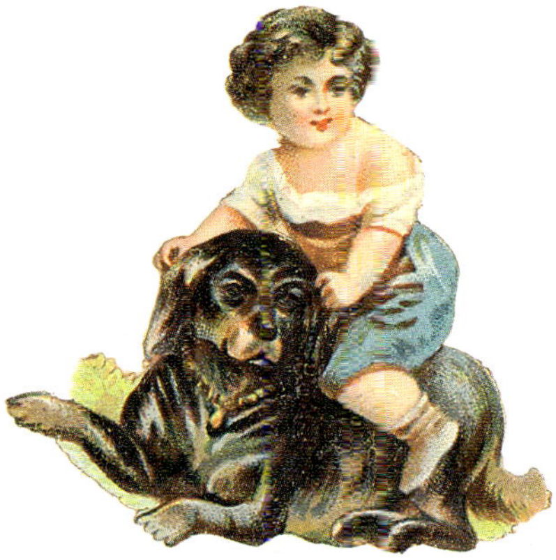
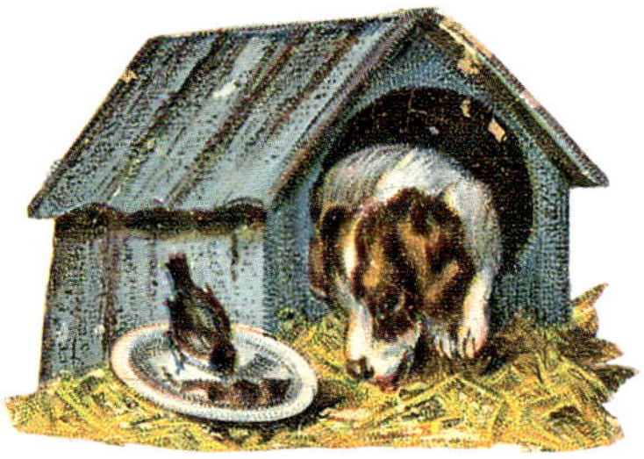
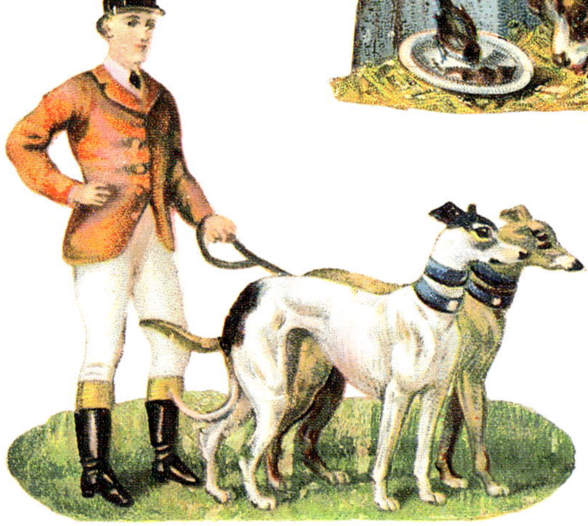
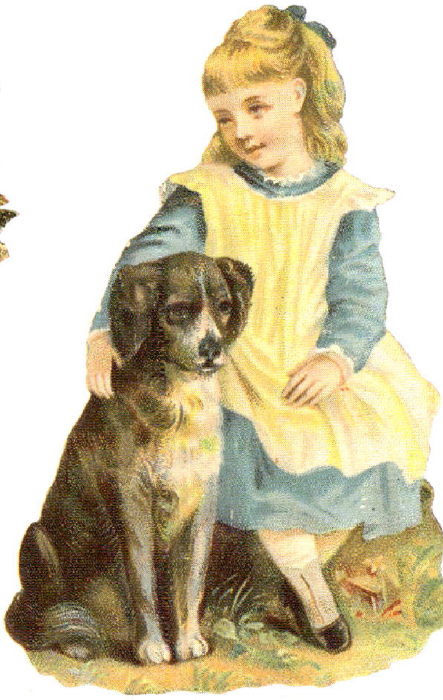
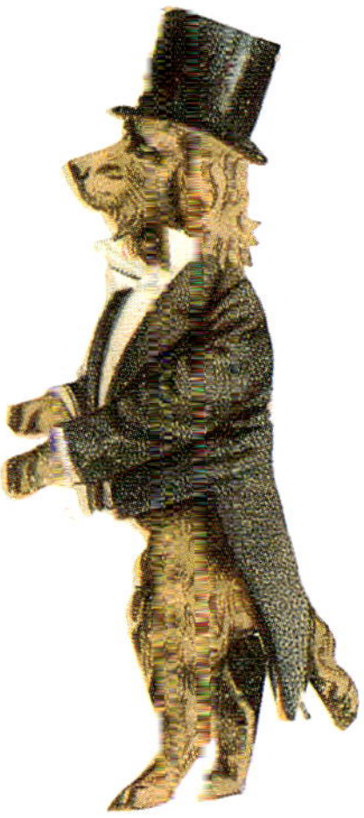

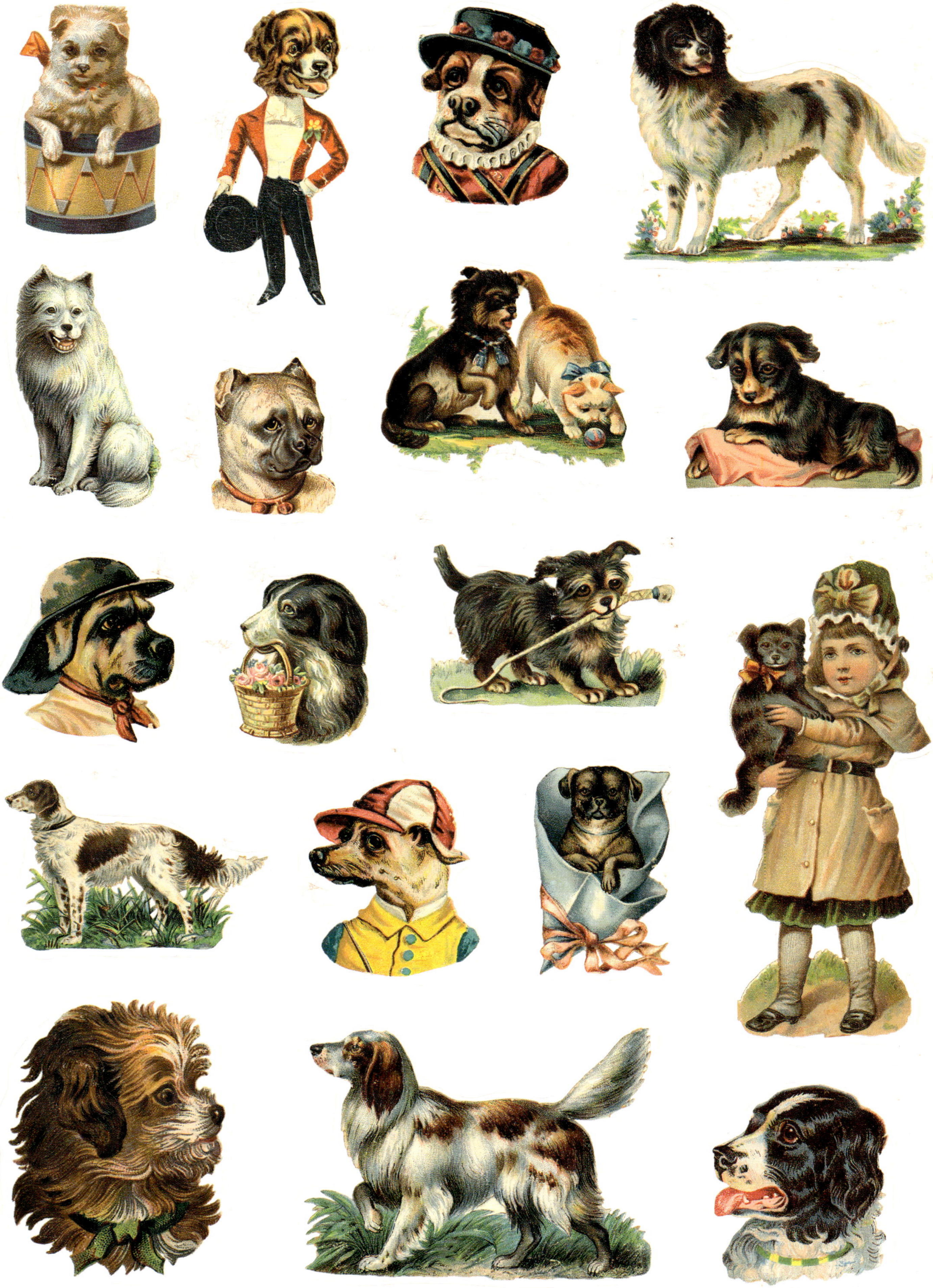

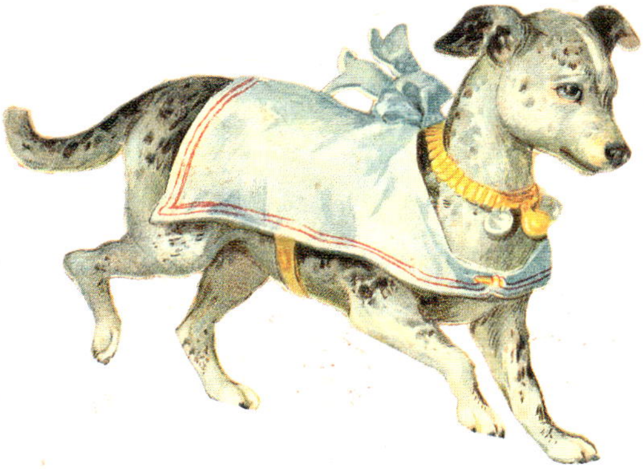
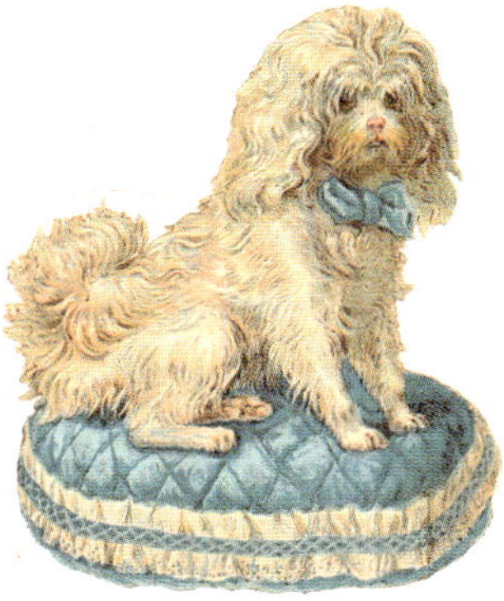
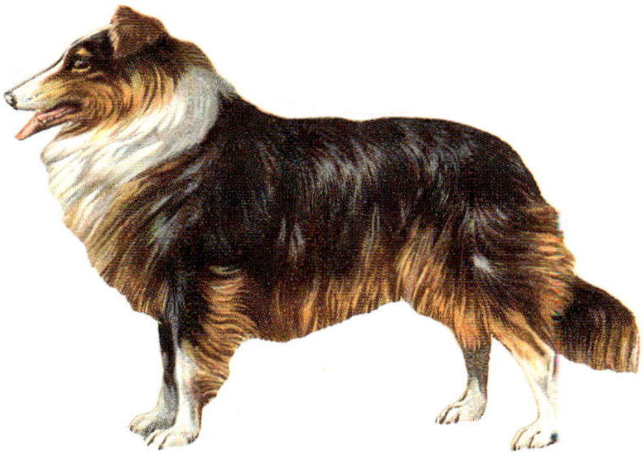
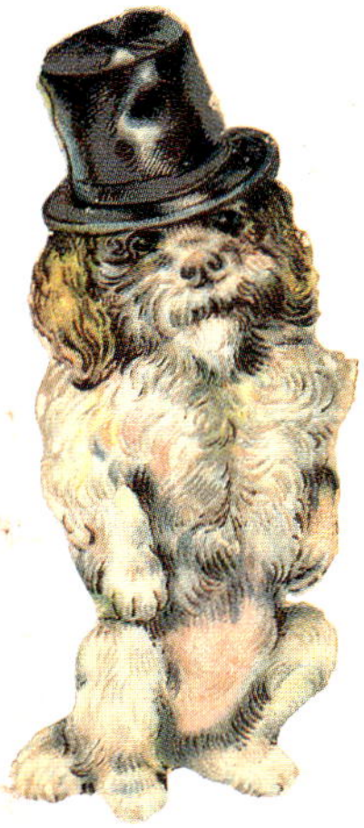
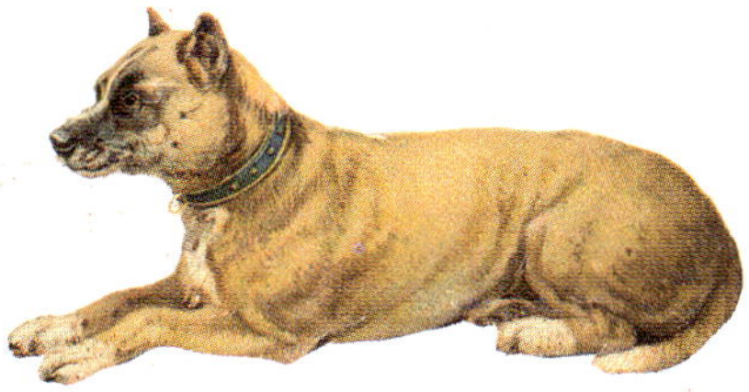
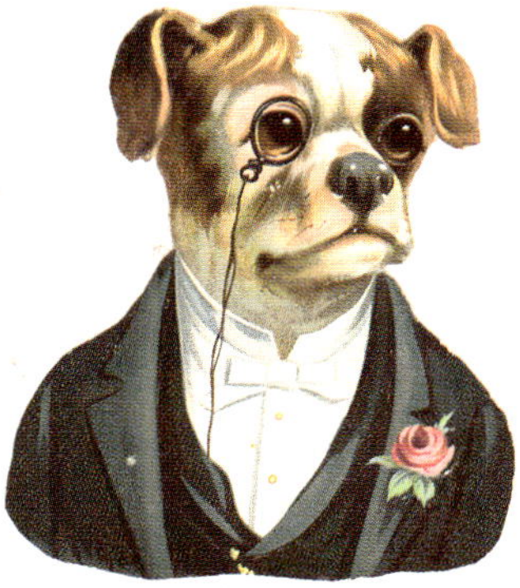
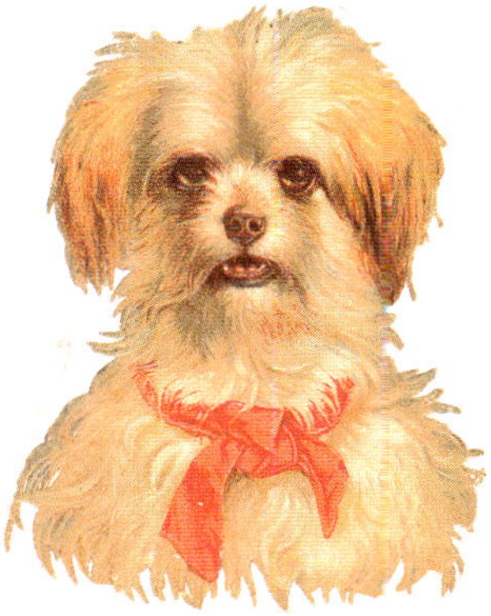
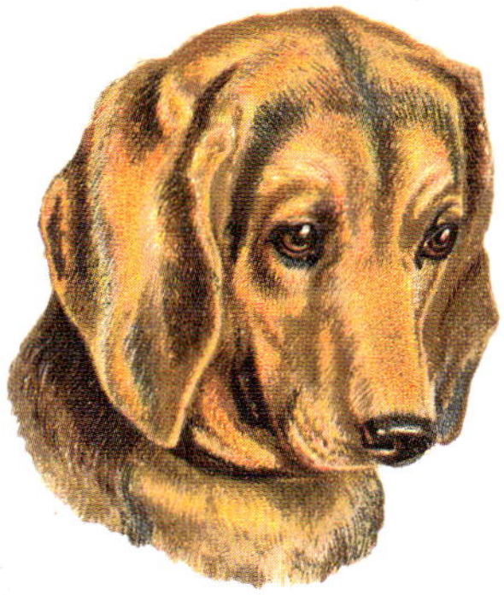
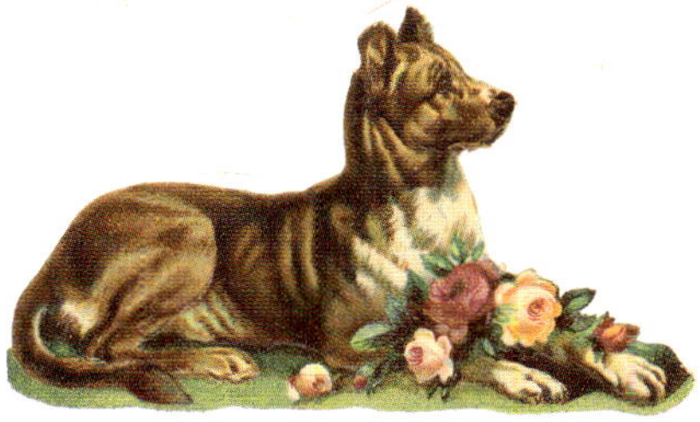
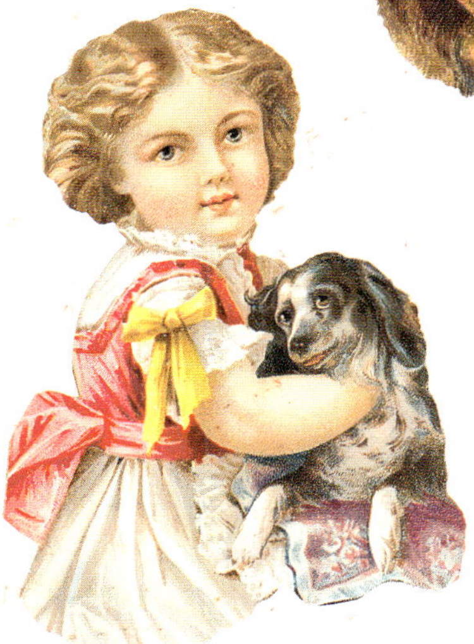
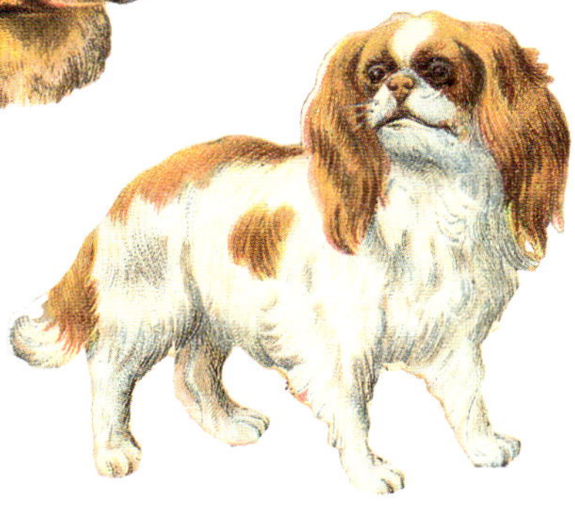
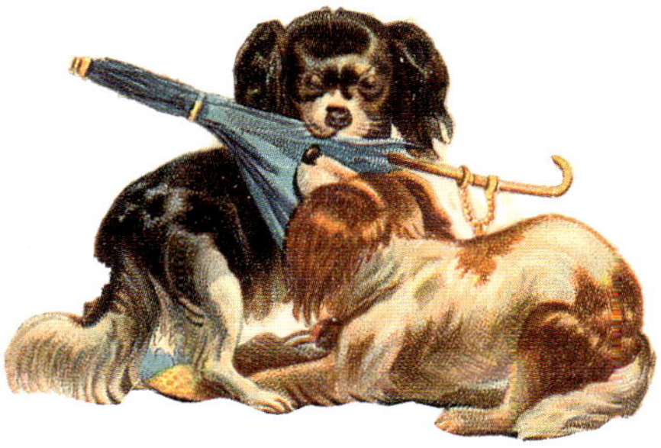
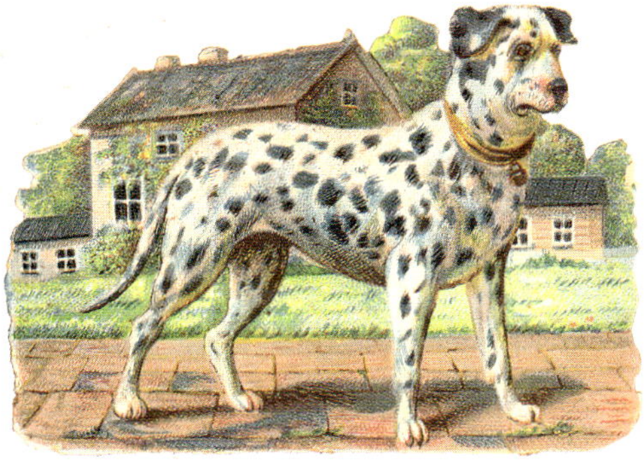
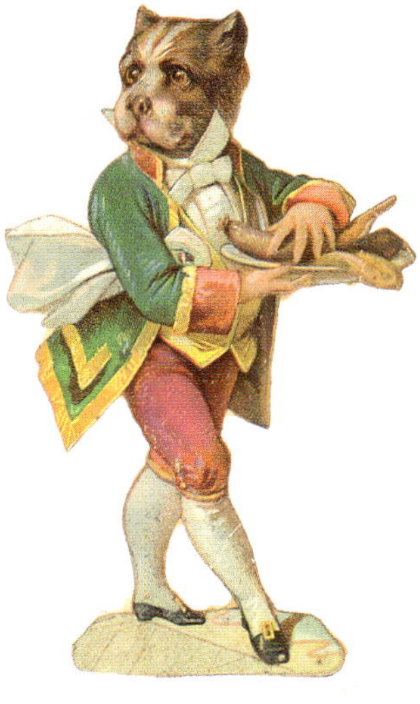
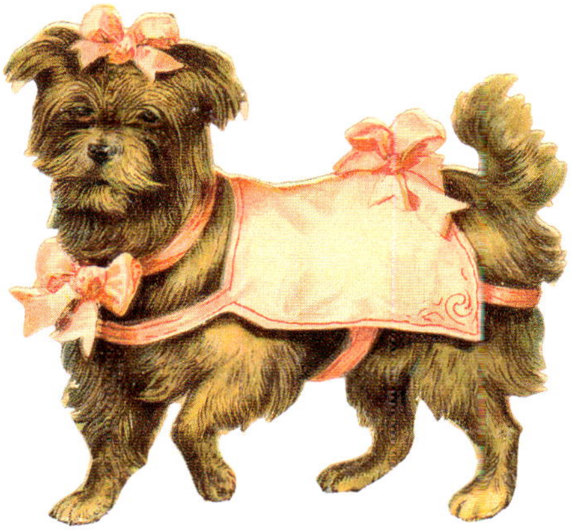

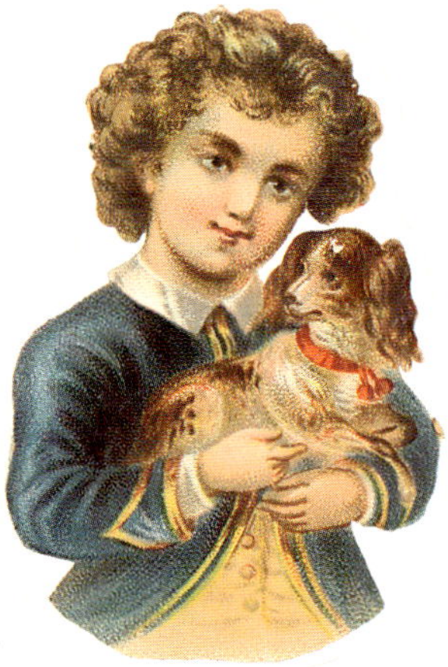
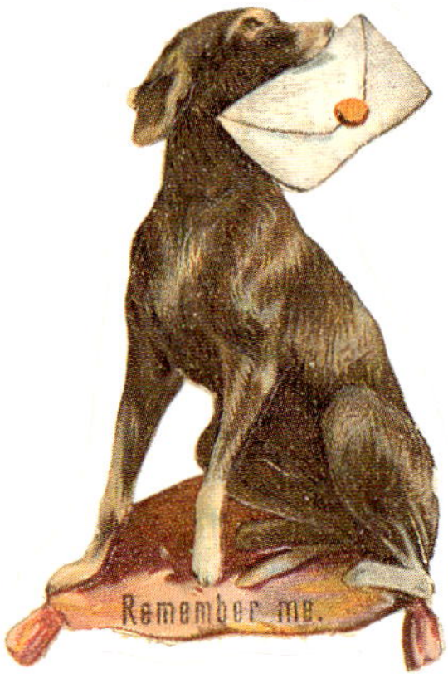
Remember me.
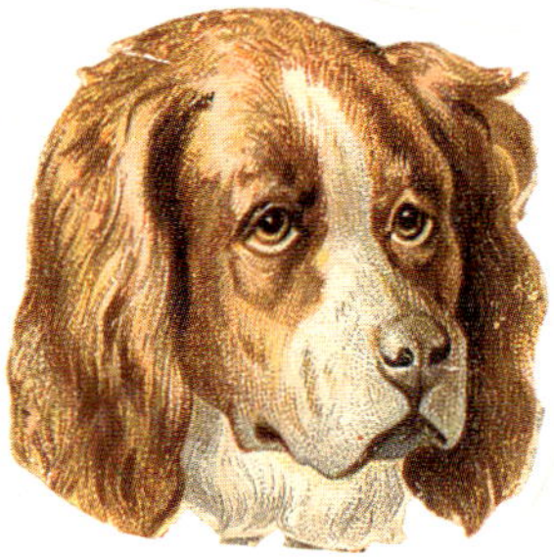
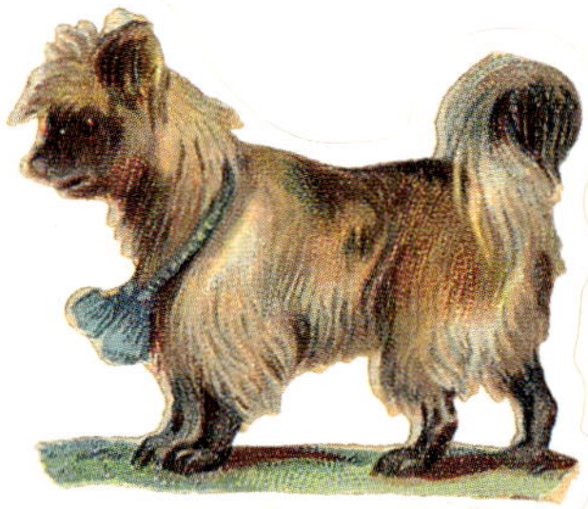
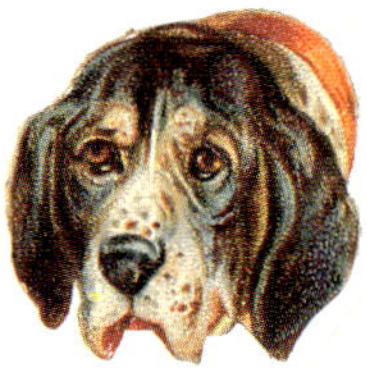
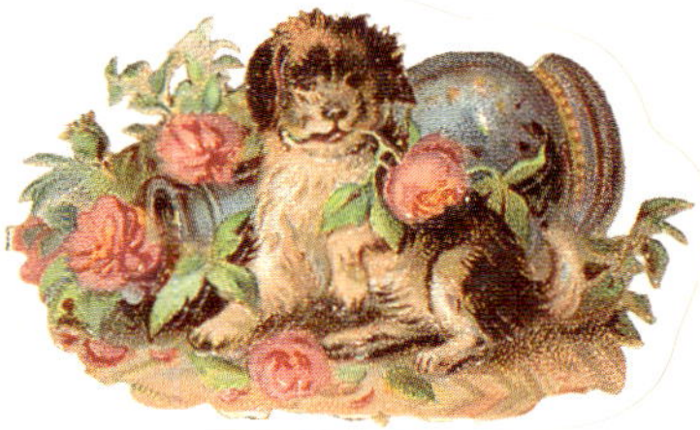
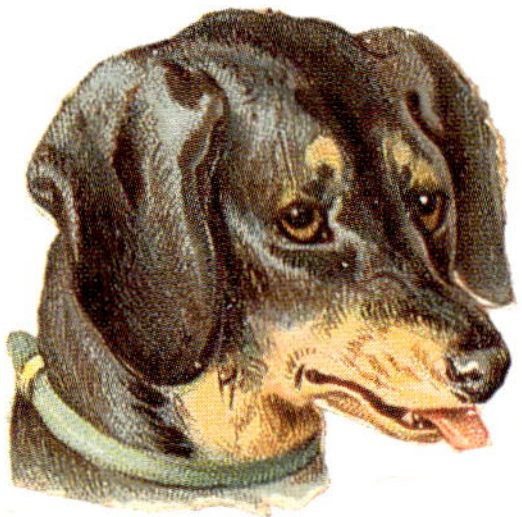
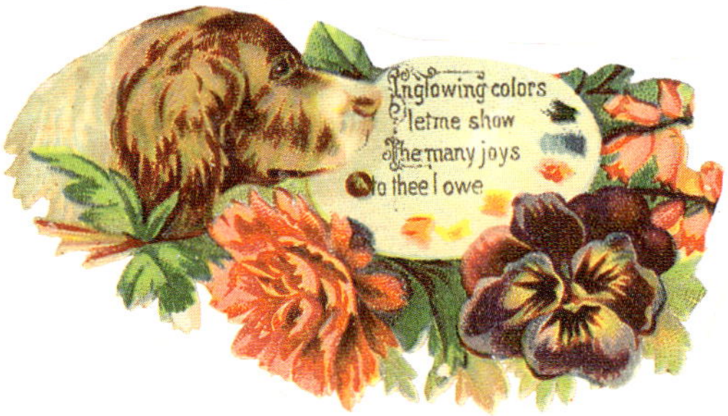
In glowing colors
let me show
The many joys
to thee I owe
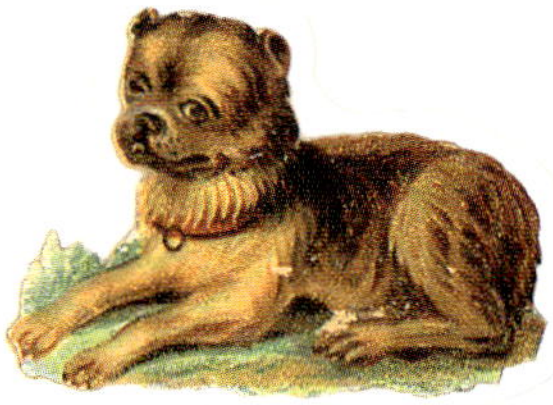
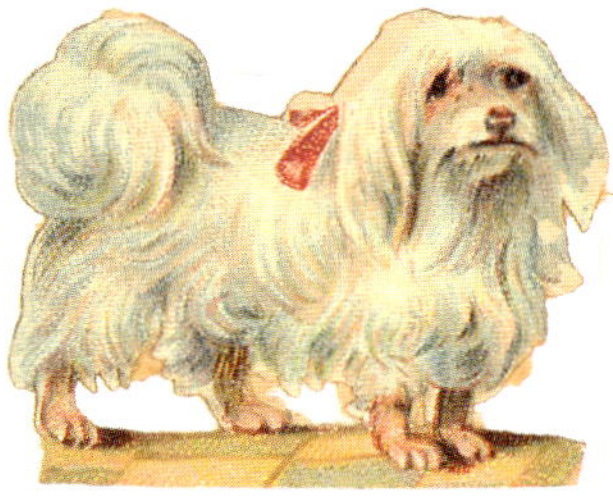
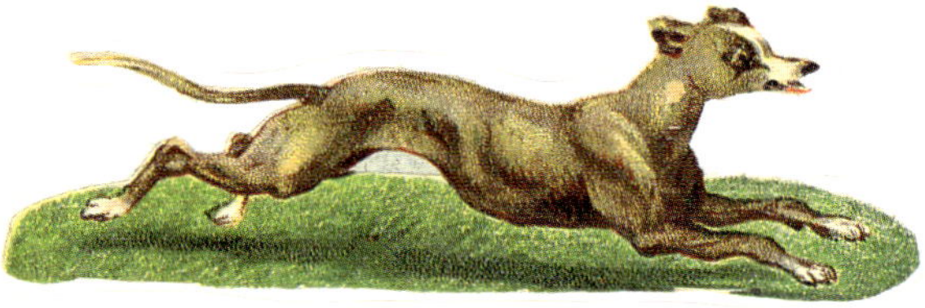
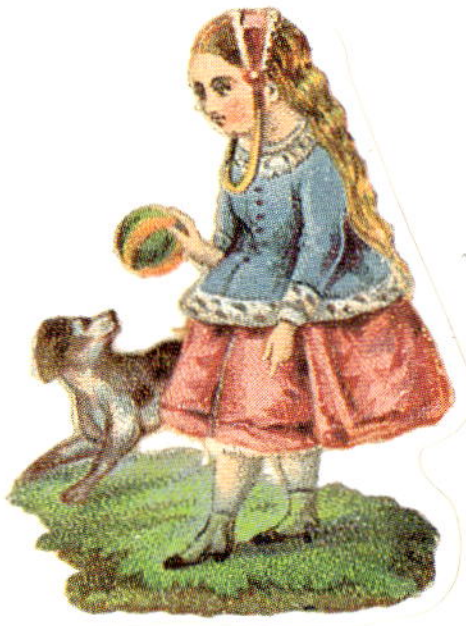
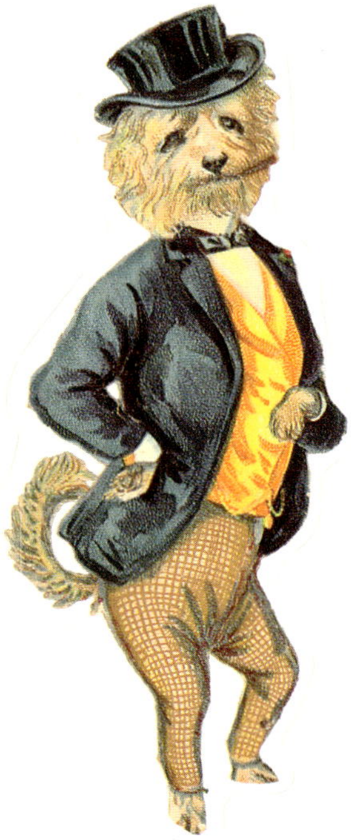
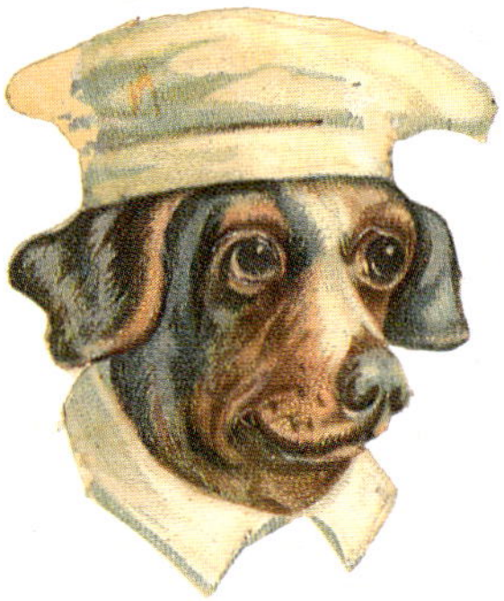
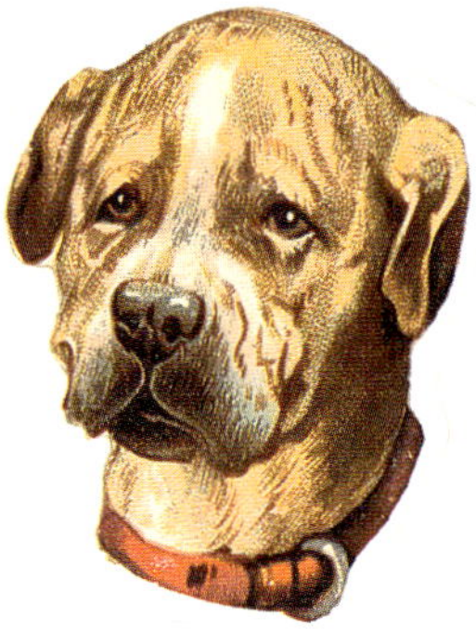
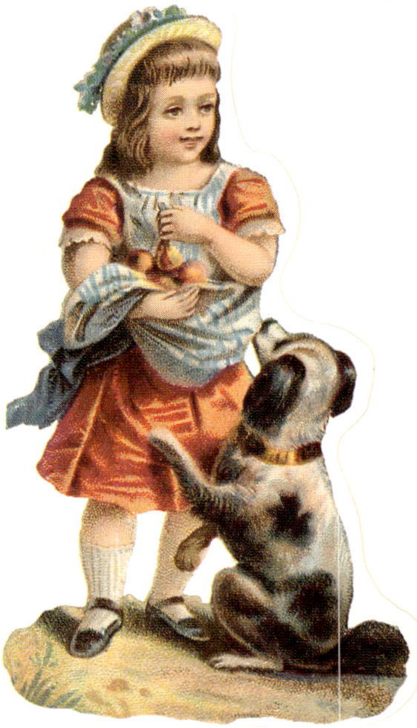
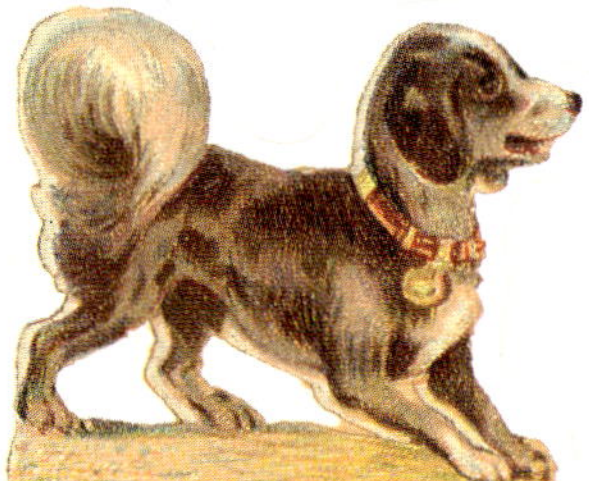
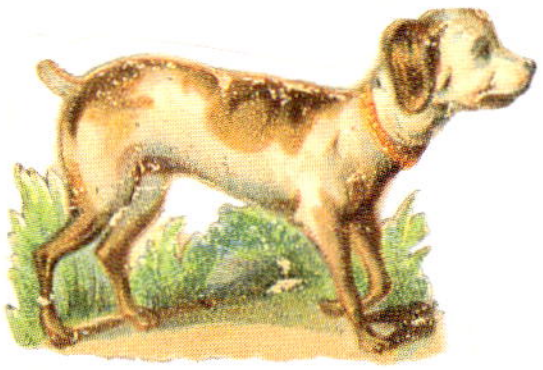

80025 75540